80 Graded Studies for Oboe

selected and edited by John Davies and Paul Harris

Book One (1–46)

CONTENTS

INTRODUCTION

In the two books comprising this collection, we have assembled a broad repertoire of study material that covers a wide spectrum of basic technique and provides a firm foundation for progress. The studies have been arranged in order of increasing difficulty, according to a carefully planned technical progression. Book One begins at elementary level, while Book Two takes the student from intermediate to advanced level.

In the main, we have drawn on established study collections by distinguished performers of the eighteenth and nineteenth centuries, all of whom made an approach to the diverse problems encountered in the development of technical facility and control. We have also included a number of new, specially composed studies that introduce aspects of twentieth-century style and thus extend the scope of the selection.

It is important to identify—perhaps with the assistance of your teacher—the specific purpose of each study and the particular facets of technique it sets out to develop. The following suggestions will be useful.

Breath control Most aspects of tonal control depend on a sustained and concentrated column of air. This is the basis of all legato and staccato playing, and a means of controlling intonation.

Tone quality It is important to maintain quality and consistency of tone when playing studies, scales and technical exercises.

Dynamics While the actual volume of sound implied by particular dynamic markings may vary from work to work, dynamic relationships within a single study should be constant. Crescendo and diminuendo should always be carefully graded, increasing or decreasing at a constant rate.

Intonation When practising studies, it is important to test intervals by reference to a tuning fork, piano or electronic tuning device.

Articulation The chosen length and quality of notes should be matched throughout and related to the character of the particular study. An understanding of the various symbols used is necessary.

Finger technique The development of a controlled and co-ordinated finger movement is the main purpose of the technical study. You should always identify the particular difficulties and seek to acquire the necessary control.

Rhythm These studies should often be practised with a metronome. Where there are rhythmic difficulties, sub-divide the basic pulse. You should always count, but it is important that undue emphasis is not placed on beats, except for a slight feeling for the natural bar accents. These primary and secondary accents should be felt but not over-emphasized.

Character The character and mood of a study should be considered, as these will determine note duration, accentuation, tone-colour and so on.

Metronome markings In most cases we have indicated the *maximum* tempo for each study. You should use your discretion regarding suggested metronome marks.

Breathing indications These are suggestions and need not be strictly observed.

The authors wish to thank Rebecca Bentley for many helpful suggestions in compiling these studies.

JOHN DAVIES & PAUL HARRIS
1990

© 1990 by Faber Music Ltd
First published in 1990 by Faber Music Ltd
Bloomsbury House 74–77 Great Russell Street London WC1B 3DA
Music engraved by Sambo Music Engraving
Cover design by Shireen Nathoo Design
Printed in England by Caligraving Ltd

ISBN10: 0-571-51175-9
EAN13: 978-0-571-51175-4

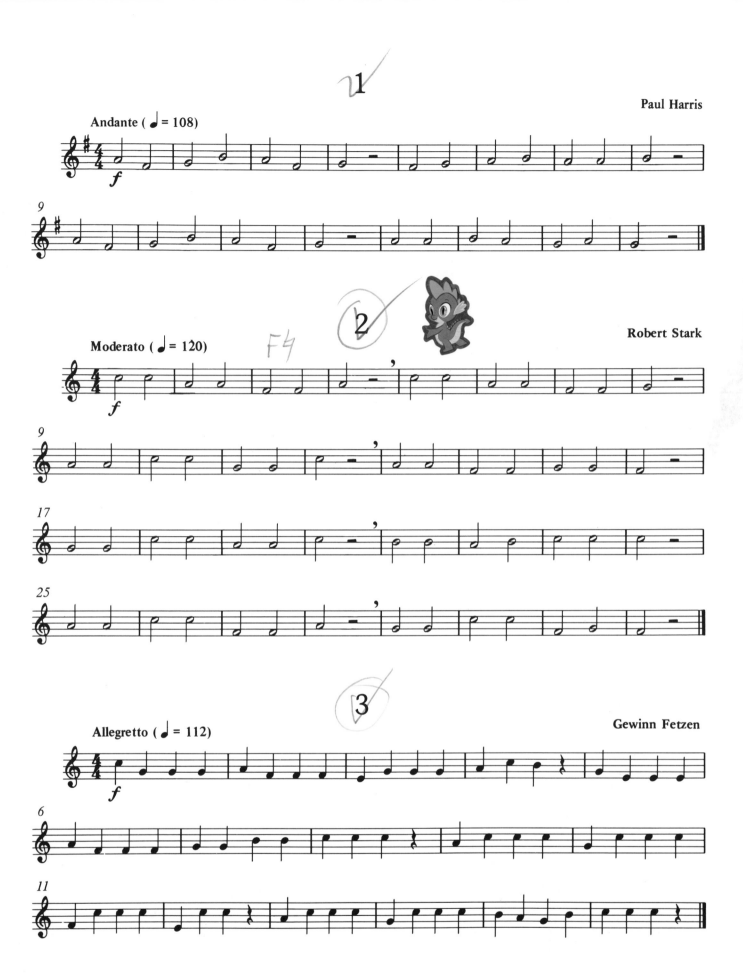

© 1990 by Faber Music Ltd.

4

Andante (♩ = 108)   Paul Harris

5

Moderato (♩ = 120)   Paul Harris

6

Andante con moto (♩ = 112)   Paul Harris

7

Con moto   Paul Harris

8

François Garnier

Andante (♩ = 104)

mf

7

p

mf

14

9

Friedrich Demnitz

Con moto (♩ = 126)

mf

8

15

f

22

10

Paul Harris

Andante (♩ = 108)

f

p

8

f

p

f

15

mp

f

11

Sostenuto (♩ = 96)

François Garnier

14

Paul Harris

15

Gewinn Fetzen

16

Henri Brod

17

Carl Baermann

18

Gustav Hinke

19

Ludwig Wiedemann

8

20

Gustav Hinke

21

François Garnier

24

Gewinn Fetzen

Maestoso (♩ = 72)

mf

poco a poco cresc.

9

f

17

rall.

dim.

25

Jean-Pierre Freillon-Poncein

Moderato (♩ = 50)

mf

f

5

p

f

10

rall.

26

Peter Prelleur

Rigaudon (♩. = 60)

f

6

11

1.

2.

27

Gustav Hinke

Tempo giusto (♩ = 100)

28

Hyacinthe Klosé

Allegro (♩ = 126)

12

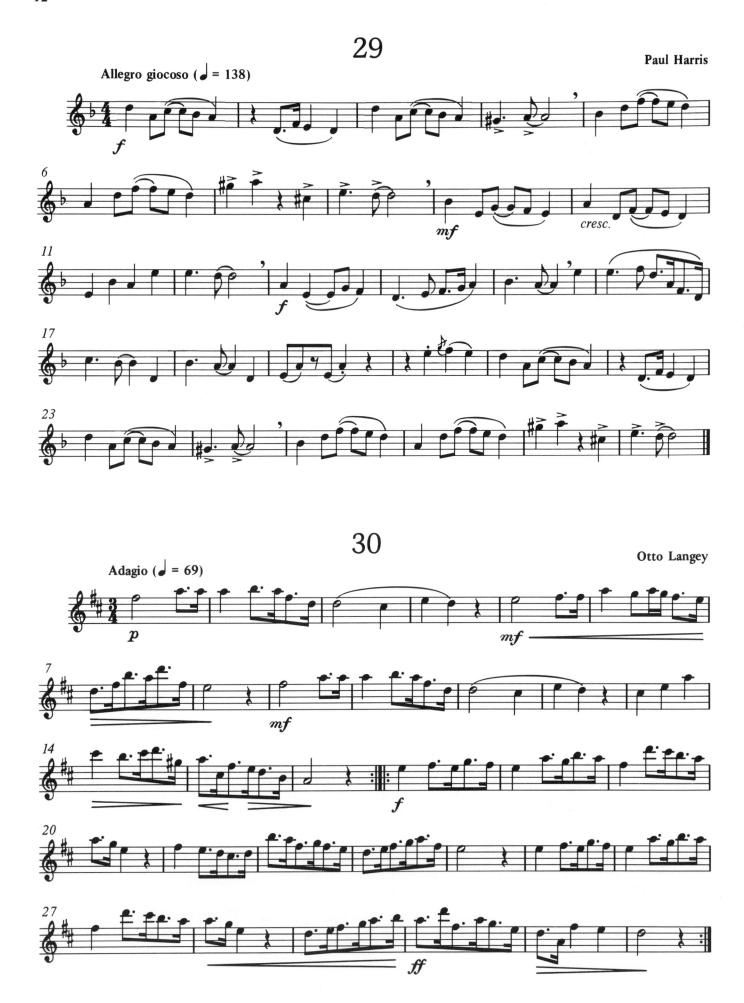

29

Paul Harris

30

Otto Langey

31

Pelham Hardy

32

François Garnier

14

33

G. Gariboldi

34

Carl Baermann

35

Paul Harris

36

Jean-Pierre Freillon-Poncein

37

Georg Wichtl

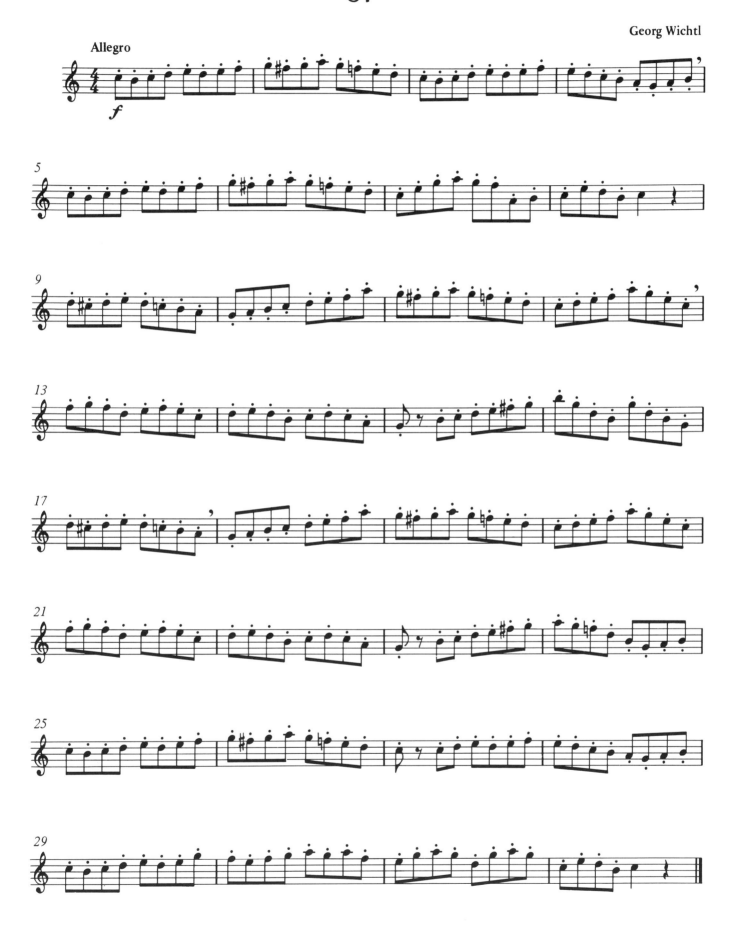

18

38

Carl Baermann

39

Henry Lazarus

Allegro moderato (♩ = 132)

40

Paul Harris

Allegro energico (♩ = 132)

41

Otto Langey

42
Csardas

Ludwig Wiedemann

43

Gustav Hinke

22

44

Gustav Hinke

Animato (♩. = 76)

45

Amand Vanderhagen

Andantino (♩ = 72)

46

Andantino (♩ = 72)

Gustav Hinke

LIST OF SOURCES

The studies in this book are drawn from the following sources:

Carl Baermann (1811–85)
Vollständige Clarinett-Schule (André, 1864–75)
(12, 17, 34, 38)
H. Brod (1799–1839)
Etudes pour Hautbois (Paris, 1835)
(16)
Friedrich Demnitz (1845–90)
Clarinetten Schule (Breitkopf & Härtel)
(9)
Gewinn Fetzen (1874–1923)
Studies (Berlin, 1983)
(3, 15, 24)
Jean-Pierre Freillon-Poncein
Le véritable manière d'apprende à jouer en perfection des hautbois, de la flûte et du flagolet (Paris, 1700)
(25, 36)
François Garnier (1759–1825)
Studienwerk für die oboe (Johann André, 1800)
(8, 11, 21, 32)

Gustav Hinke
Praktische Elementarschule (Leipzig, 1888)
(13, 18, 20, 27, 43, 44, 46)
Hyacinthe Klosé (1808–80)
Méthode Complète de Clarinette (Meissonnier, 1843)
(28)
Otto Langey (1851–1922)
The Saxophone (Hawkes and Sons, 1927)
(23, 30, 41)
Henry Lazarus (1815–95)
New and Modern Method (Lafleur, 1881)
(39)
Peter Prelleur (?–1750)
Instructions upon the Hautboy in a more familiar method than any extant (London, 1731)
(26)
Robert Stark (1847–1922)
Practical Staccato School, op.53 (Benjamin, 1909)
(2)
Ludwig Wiedemann (1856–1918)
30 Studies (Breitkopf & Härtel)
(19, 42)

GLOSSARY OF TERMS

A tempo	Resume the original tempo	*Larghetto*	Slow and dignified
Accelerando (accel.)	Becoming faster	*Largo*	Slowly
Adagio	Slow	*Legato*	Smoothly
Allegretto	A little slower than *Allegro*	*Leggiero*	Lightly
Allegro	Lively	*Lento*	Slow
Allargando (allarg.)	Broadening	*Marcato (marc.)*	Marked
Andante	lit. 'at a walking pace'	*Meno*	Less
Andantino	Slower than *Andante*	*Mesto*	Sadly
Animato	Animated	*Moderato*	At a moderate pace
Assai	Very, extremely	*Moto*	Movement
Brillante	Brilliant	*Non troppo*	Not too much
Calando	Dying away	*Più*	More
Cantabile (cant.)	In a singing style	*Poco*	Little
Con	With	*Presto*	Fast
Con brio	With spirit	*Rallentando (rall.)*	Becoming gradually slower
Crescendo (cresc.)	Becoming louder	*Religioso*	Solemnly
Diminuendo (dim.)	Becoming softer	*Ritardando (rit.)*	Held back
Delicato	Delicately	*Scherzando*	Playfully, lightly
Dolce	Sweetly	*Sempre*	Always
e	And	*Simile (sim.)*	In the same manner
Energico	Energetically	*Sostenuto*	Sustained
Fuoco	Fire	*Staccato (stacc.)*	Short and detached
Giocoso	Jocular	*Tempo giusto*	In strict time
Grave	Very slow	*Vigoroso*	Vigorously
Gusto	Vigour	*Vivando*	With life